Helping Our World

By Michele Spirn

Scott Foresman
is an imprint of

Glenview, Illinois • Boston, Massachusetts • Chandler, Arizona •
Upper Saddle River, New Jersey

Photographs

Every effort has been made to secure permission and provide appropriate credit for photographic material. The publisher deeply regrets any omission and pledges to correct errors called to its attention in subsequent editions.

Unless otherwise acknowledged, all photographs are the property of Pearson Education, Inc.

Photo locators denoted as follows: Top (T), Center (C), Bottom (B), Left (L), Right (R), Background (Bkgd)

CVR Jose Luis Pelaez, Inc./Corbis; **1** Richard Hutchings/PhotoEdit, Inc.; **4** ©Leland BobbŽ/ Corbis; **5** ©ONOKY - Photononstop/Alamy; **6** ©GoGo Images Corporation/Alamy; **7** Richard Hutchings/PhotoEdit, Inc.; **8** Jose Luis Pelaez, Inc./Corbis

ISBN 13: 978-0-328-46353-4
ISBN 10:   0-328-46353-1

You can help our world.
You can help in many ways.

You can help make our world cleaner.
You can pick up your trash.

You can help our world
save water.
Turn off the water if you
don't need it.

You can help our world save energy.
Turn off the TV when you are not watching it.

Walk to school if you can.
Ride your bike when you can.
This will save energy and
keep the air clean.

Plant a tree.

Trees make our air cleaner.

You can help our world in
many ways.

. . . .

Is there ANYTHING...
to beat finding yourself
at large in a
foreign city on a fair spring
evening, loafing along
unfamiliar streets in the long
shadows of a lazy sunset,
pausing to gaze in shop
windows or at some church or
lovely square or tranquil
stretch of quayside...

-Bill Bryson

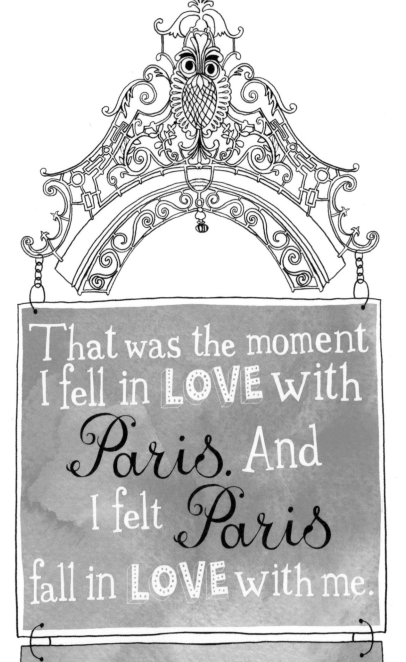

That was the moment I fell in **LOVE** with *Paris.* And I felt *Paris* fall in **LOVE** with me.

—2006 film *Paris, je t'aime*

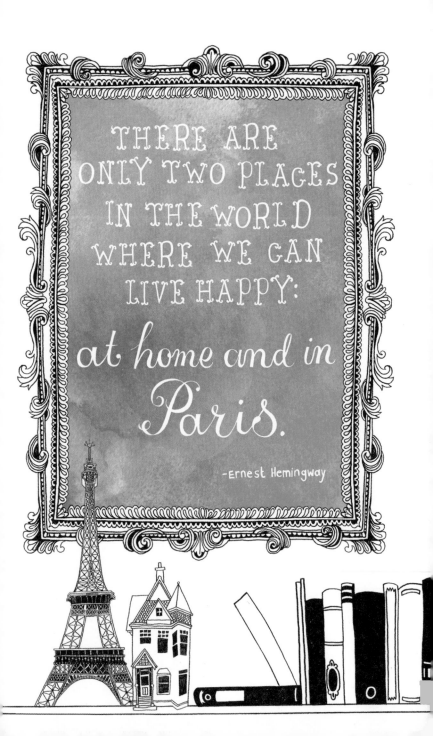

THERE ARE ONLY TWO PLACES IN THE WORLD WHERE WE CAN LIVE HAPPY:

at home and in Paris.

-Ernest Hemingway

Give me books, French wine, fruit, fine weather and a little music played out of doors by somebody I do not know.

– John keats

...we can just **ACCEPT**

the fact that we were made for

Paris!

— C. JoyBell C.